IN RECITAL® WITH *Timeless Hymns*

(IN A CONTEMPORARY SETTING)

ABOUT THE SERIES • A NOTE TO THE TEACHER

In Recital® with Timeless Hymns is devoted to everlasting hymns that have been sung and heard throughout many generations. The outstanding arrangers of this series have created engaging arrangements of these hymns, which have been carefully leveled to ensure success. We know that to motivate, the teacher must challenge the student with attainable goals. This series makes that possible while also providing peaceful and joyous musical settings for your students. You will find favorites that are easy to sing along with, as well as recital-style arrangements. This series complements other FJH publications, and will help you plan student performances throughout the years. The books include CDs with complete performances designed to assist with performance preparation as well as for pure listening pleasure. Throughout this series you will find interesting background information for Hymns by Lyndell Leatherman.

Use the enclosed CD as a teaching and motivational tool. For a guide to listening to the CD, turn to page 44.

Production: Frank J. Hackinson
Production Coordinators: Joyce Loke and Satish Bhakta
Cover Design: Terpstra Design, San Francisco, CA
Cover Illustration: Keith Alexander
Engraving: Tempo Music Press, Inc.
Printer: Tempo Music Press, Inc.

ISBN-13: 978-1-56939-919-4

ORGANIZATION OF THE SERIES
IN RECITAL® WITH TIMELESS HYMNS

The series is carefully leveled into the following six categories: Early Elementary, Elementary, Late Elementary, Early Intermediate, Intermediate, and Late Intermediate. Each of the works has been selected for its artistic as well as its pedagogical merit.

Book Three — Late Elementary, reinforces the following concepts:

- Eighth notes and dotted quarter notes are added to the basic notes students played in books 1 and 2.

- Students play different articulations such as *legato* and *staccato* at the same time.

- Melodies are played in the left as well as the right hand.

- Students play pieces in a variety of different moods and tempos.

- Pieces reinforce five-finger scales, as well as scale patterns that extend from the usual five-finger patterns (with finger crossings).

- Blocked intervals up to a sixth and double thirds.

- Students use the pedal to create a big sound as well as to play artistically.

- Keys of C major, G major, F major, and D minor.

Praise to the Lord, the Almighty was arranged as an unequal-part duet and *Poor Wayfaring Stranger* was arranged as an equal-part duet. The rest of the selections are solos.

TABLE OF CONTENTS

FJH2144

ABOUT THE PIECES AND COMPOSERS

Onward Christian Soldiers

In mid 19th-century England, the religious holiday known as Whitsun (White Sunday) was celebrated in the Anglican Church by children parading through the streets carrying banners and following a leader who carried a cross.

In 1864, as was the custom in the Horbury Bridge, Yorkshire parish, the children's procession was scheduled to march to a neighboring village on Whitmon (the day after Whitsun), where they would attend a Sunday School rally. Their pastor, Sabine Baring-Gould (1834-1924) had a last-minute inspiration: their long walk would be less tiring if they had a suitable marching song to sing. The evening before, he had searched the church's hymnbook for something suitable, but found nothing. So laboring most of the night, he created a text which he called *Hymn for Procession with Cross and Banners*-sung to the familiar theme of the slow movement of Haydn's *Symphony in D*. Seven years later it was reset to the tune we know today by a famous English organist, Sir Arthur S. Sullivan, and given its new name, *Onward Christian Soldiers*.

I Need Thee Every Hour

Annie Sherwood Hawks (1835-1918) was born in Hoosick, New York. Early in life she displayed an unusual talent for creative writing, and at the age of fourteen began seeing her poetry printed in newspapers. After marrying she moved to Brooklyn, New York, where she joined a Baptist church. Her pastor at that time was Robert Lowry, a well-known composer of gospel songs. Upon learning of her writing skills, he encouraged her to write hymns. One Sunday in 1872 she handed him a poem titled *I Need Thee Every Hour*. Lowry set the lyrics to music and added a refrain (chorus). The new hymn was included in a small collection, *Gospel Songs*, compiled for use by the National Baptist Sunday School Association in their national convention later that year in Cincinnati, Ohio. There the song was warmly received and quickly spread around the country.

ABOUT THE PIECES AND COMPOSERS

We Gather Together

The anonymous Dutch hymn text later translated as *We Gather Together* was probably written around 1600. For over 200 years the song was mostly sung only by the Dutch people, who used it as a patriotic song. In 1877 Edward Kremser, an Austrian conductor and composer, discovered the song with a German translation and was inspired to arrange it for men's choir. From Austria the song found its way to Milwaukee, Wisconsin around 1895, where it became a favorite among the German-speaking community there.

Theodore Baker was a well-respected scholar who enjoyed a thirty-four year career as a music editor for G. Schirmer, Inc. He is perhaps best known for his dictionaries of musicians and musical terms, still in use today. Baker translated *We Gather Together* into English and included it in a collection titled *Dutch Folk Songs,* which was published in 1917. Since then it has become one of America's favorite Thanksgiving hymns.

Praise to the Lord, the Almighty

Joachim Neander was born in Germany in 1650. His father, grandfather, and great-grandfather were all ministers. While he was a college student, he rejected his family's values and became very wicked. One day as he walked past a church service in progress, he decided to go inside and heckle the new preacher. However, the words of the minister were so powerful that Joachim instead decided to turn his life around and serve God. After graduating from college, he taught for a while before returning to that same church to serve as an assistant to the minister who had been so influential in his life. Before too long he became very ill and died after several months. But in his last year of life he managed to write several hymn texts, the most famous of which was *Praise to the Lord, the Almighty.* Almost 200 years later, Catherine Winkworth translated Neander's German lyrics into English.

Shall We Gather at the River

Robert Lowry (1826-1899) was born in Philadelphia, Pennsylvania. He attended the University of Lewisburg (later renamed Bucknell University), and then for a while taught literature there. After being ordained as a Baptist minister, he pastored churches in Pennsylvania, New York, and New Jersey. Along the way he wrote approximately 500 hymn texts or tunes. Although he had no formal training in music composition, he had an amazing ability to write memorable songs such as *Shall We Gather at the River.*

Onward Christian Soldiers

Music by Arthur S. Sullivan
Lyrics by Sabine Baring-Gould
arr. Robert Schultz

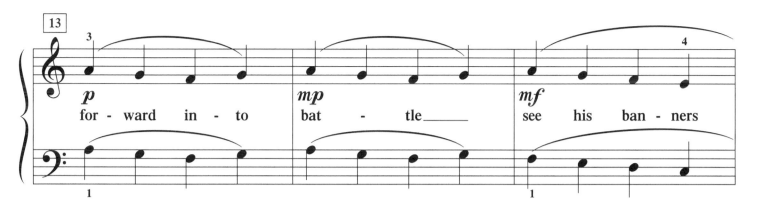

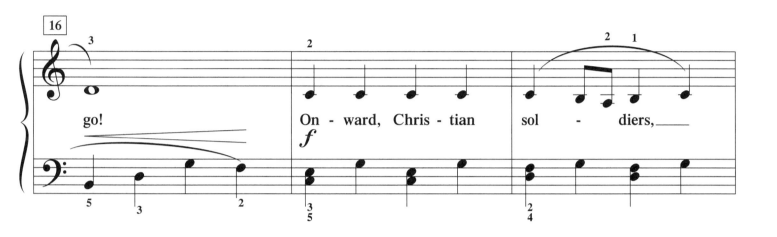

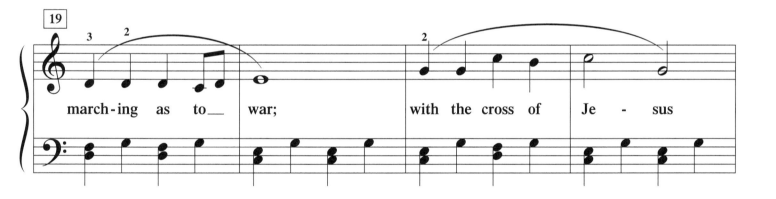

I Need Thee Every Hour

Music by Robert Lowry
Lyrics by Annie S. Hawks
arr. Edwin McLean

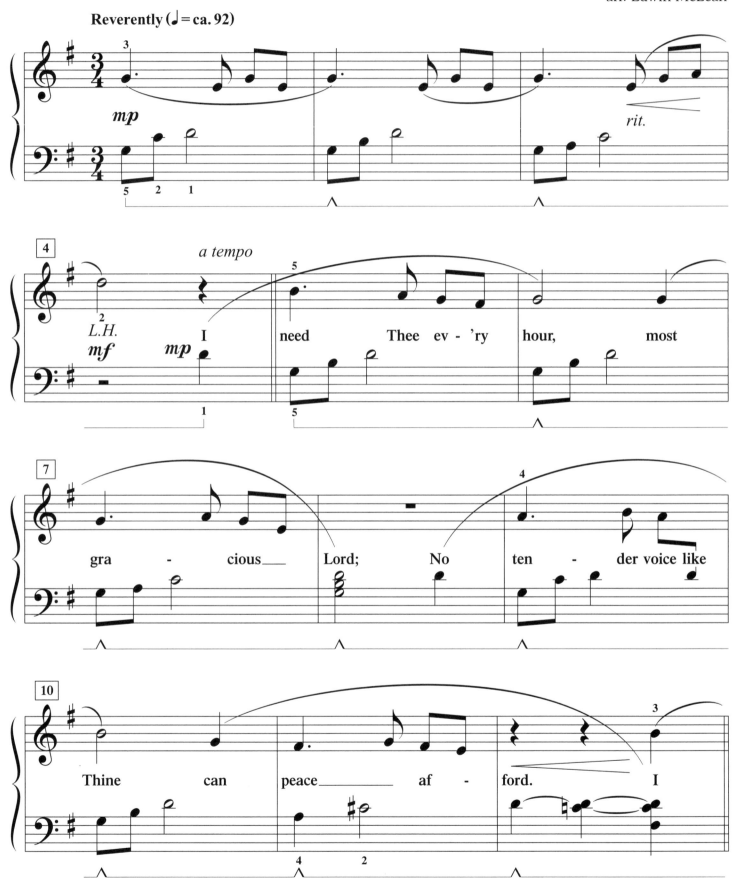

We Gather Together

Dutch Folk Hymn
Lyrics translated by Theodore Baker
arr. Nancy Lau

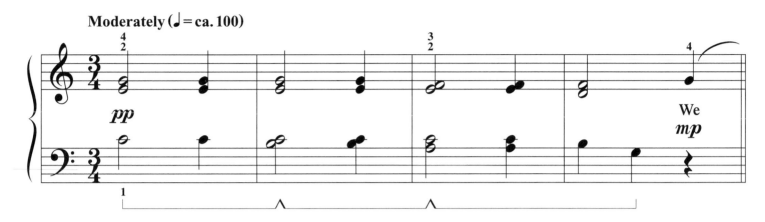

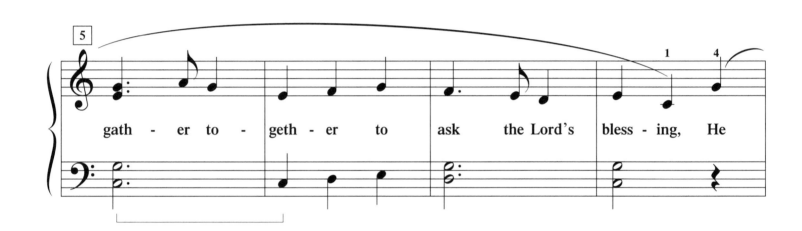

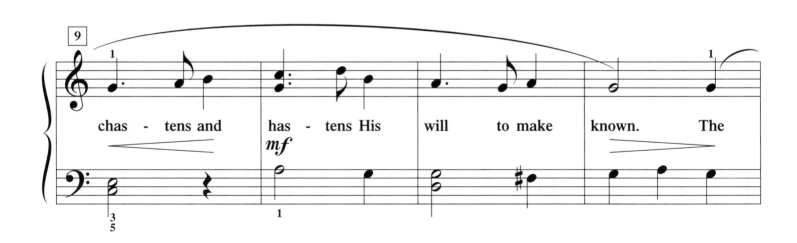

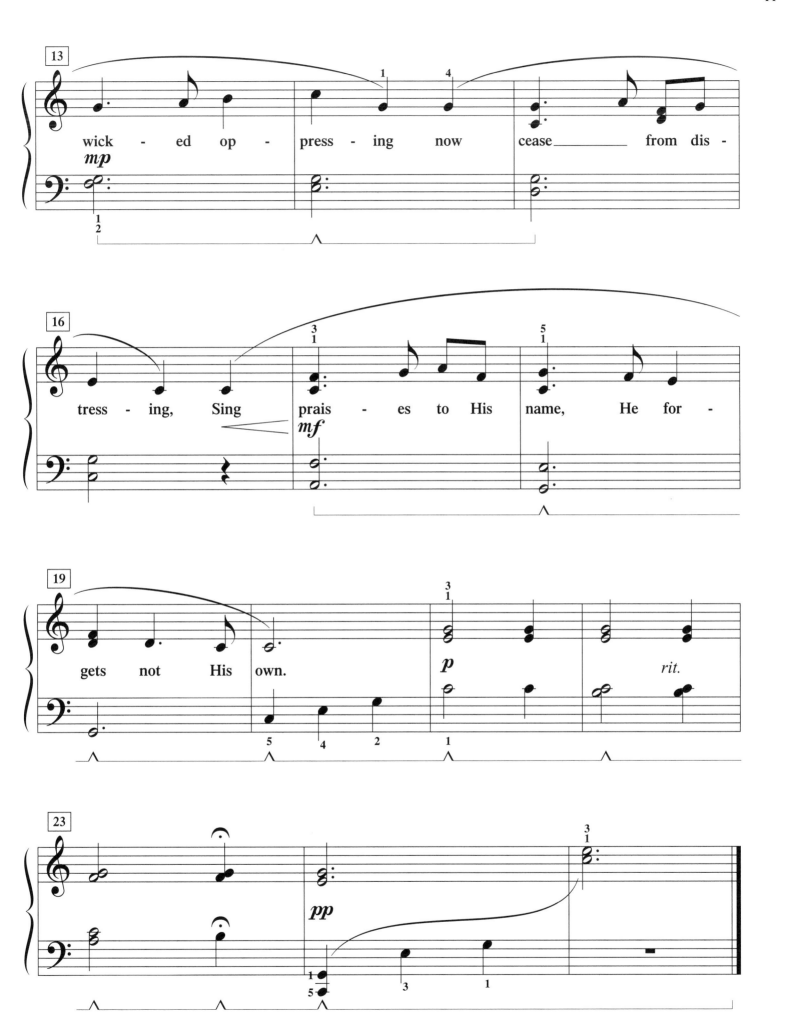

Praise to the Lord, the Almighty
Secondo
Teacher Part

Music from *Erneuerten Gesangbuch*
arr. Edwin McLean

Praise to the Lord, the Almighty

Primo
Student Part

Music from *Erneuerten Gesangbuch*
arr. Edwin McLean

Play both hands 8va higher throughout

Moderately; expressively (♩ = ca. 84)

Secondo
Teacher Part

Primo
Student Part

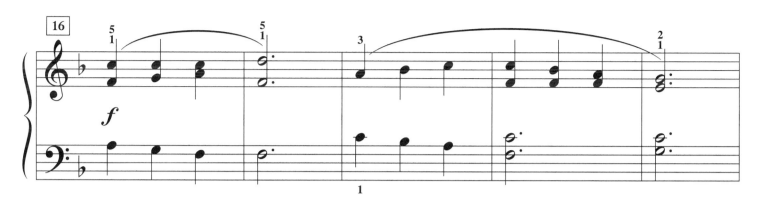

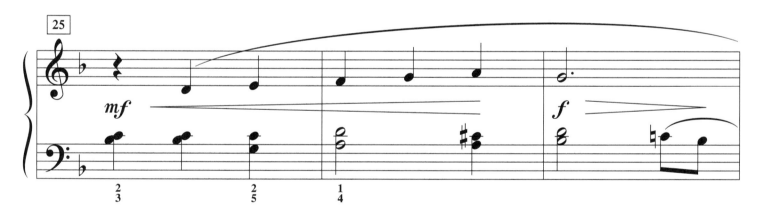

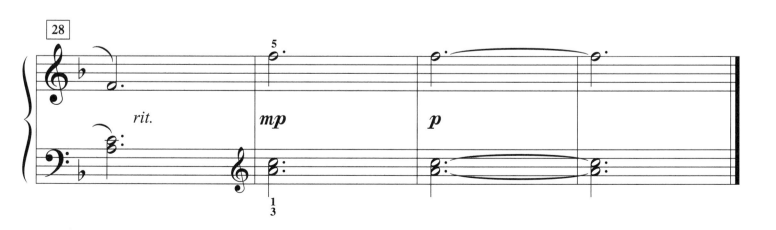

FJH2144

Shall We Gather at the River

Robert Lowry
arr. Robert Schultz

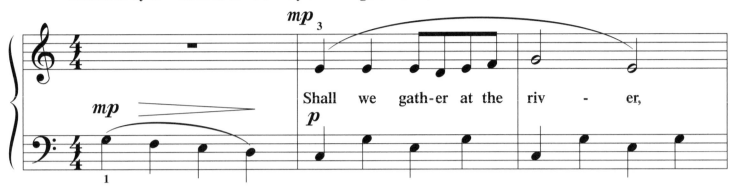

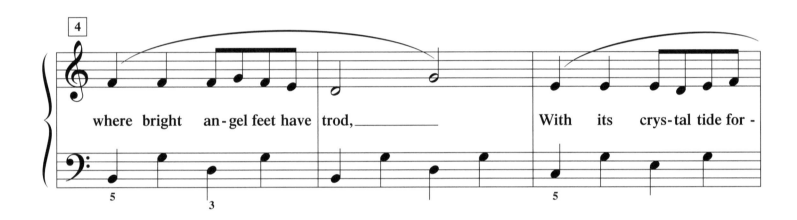

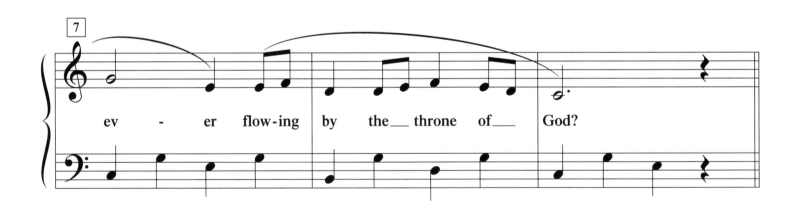

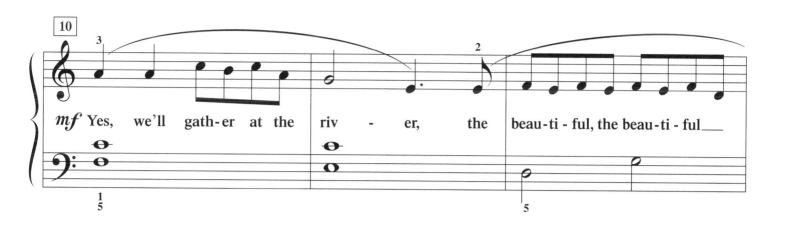

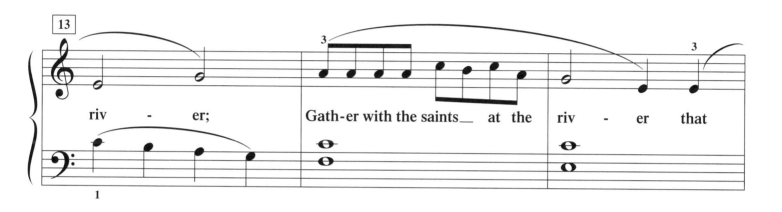

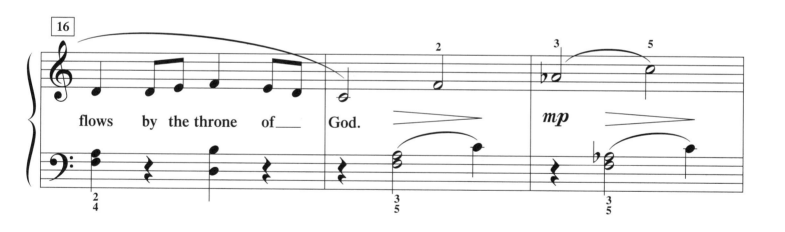

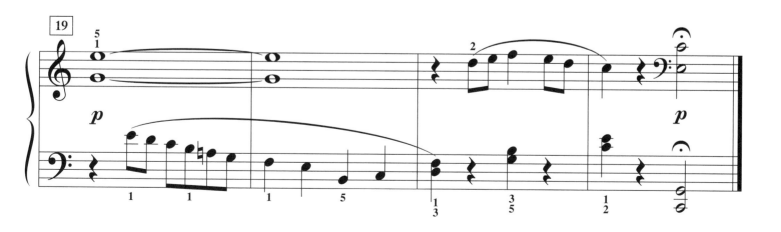

Just a Closer Walk with Thee

Anonymous
arr. Edwin McLean

God Be with You

Music by William G. Tomer
Lyrics by Jeremiah E. Rankin
arr. Nancy Lau

FJH2144

What Wondrous Love Is This

American Folk Hymn
arr. Valerie Roth Roubos

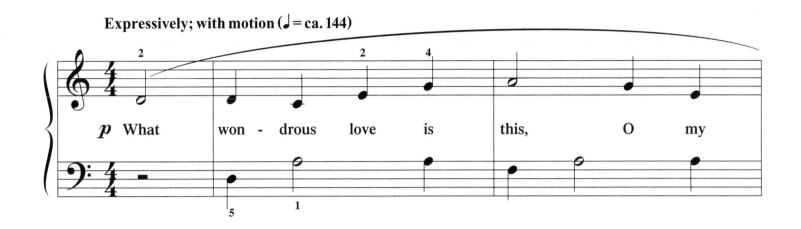

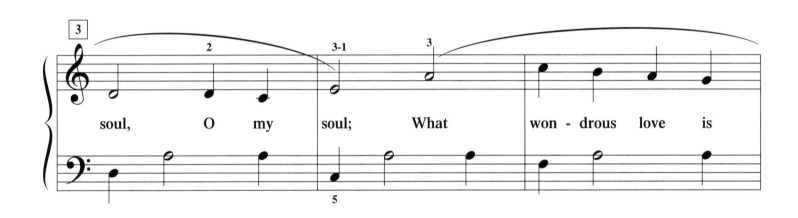

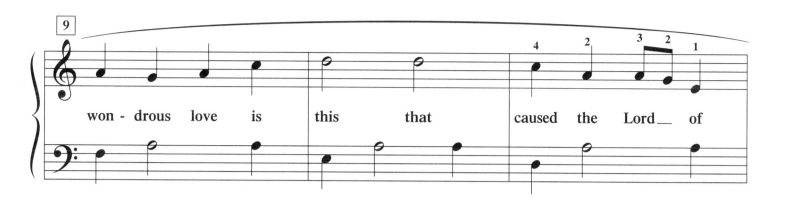

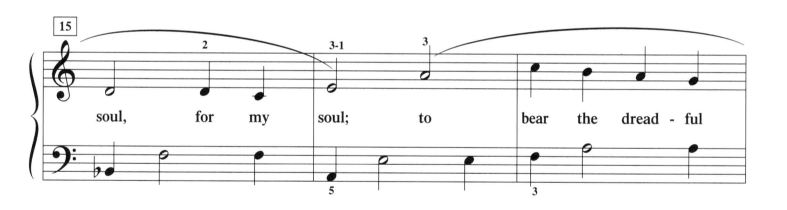

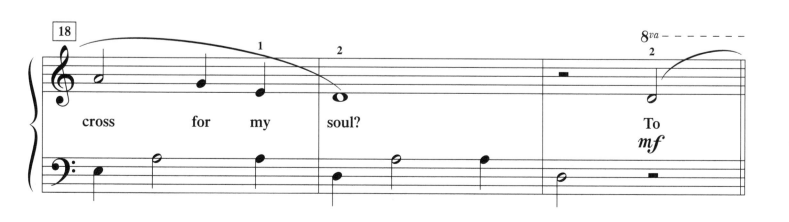

God and to the Lamb I will sing, I will

sing; to God and to the Lamb I will

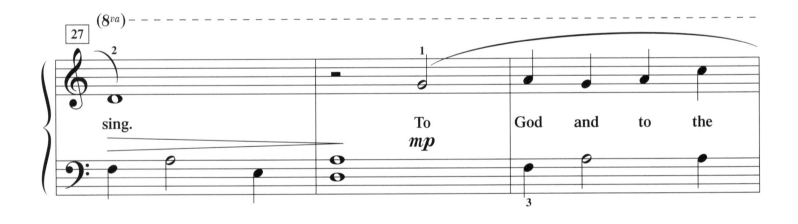

sing. To God and to the
mp

Lamb who is the great "I Am,"
mf

25

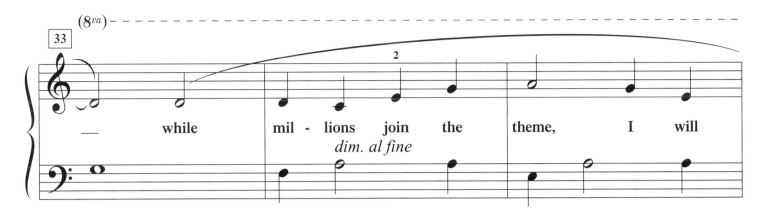

while mil - lions join the theme, I will

dim. al fine

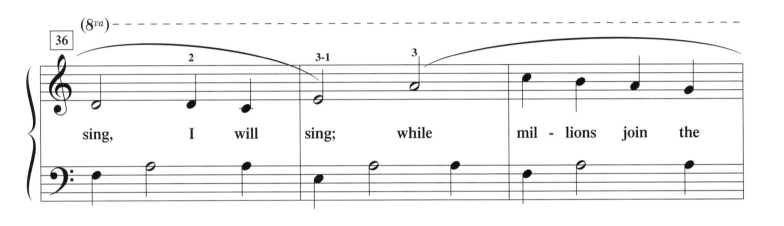

sing, I will sing; while mil - lions join the

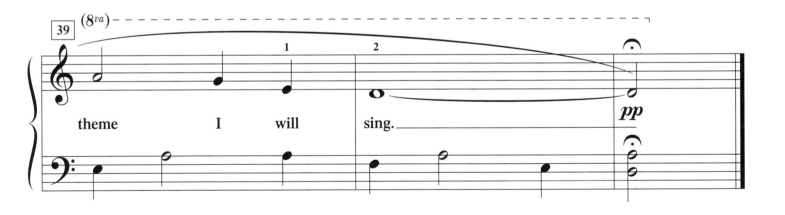

theme I will sing.

pp

25

25

FJH2144

Rock of Ages

Music by Thomas Hastings
Lyrics by Augustus M. Toplady
arr. Valerie Roth Roubos

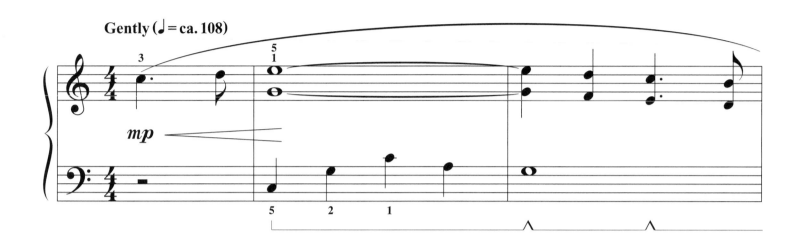

Rock of A - ges,

cleft for me, Let me

Lyrics: hide myself in Thee; Let the water and the blood, From Thy wounded side which flowed, Be of

28

FJH2144

For the Beauty of the Earth

Music by Conrad Kocher
Lyrics by Folliott S. Pierpont
arr. Nancy Lau

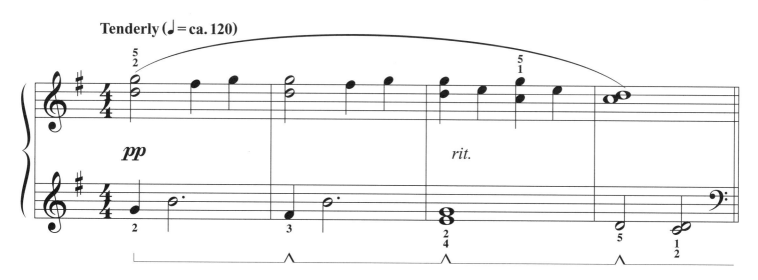

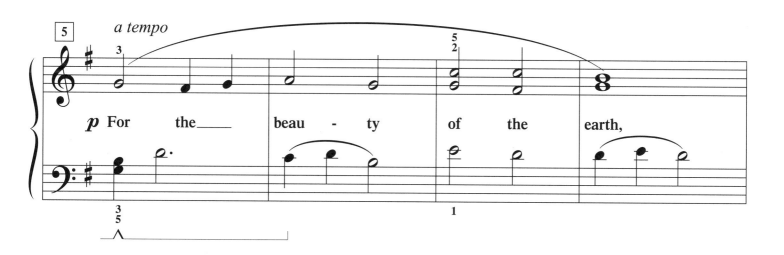

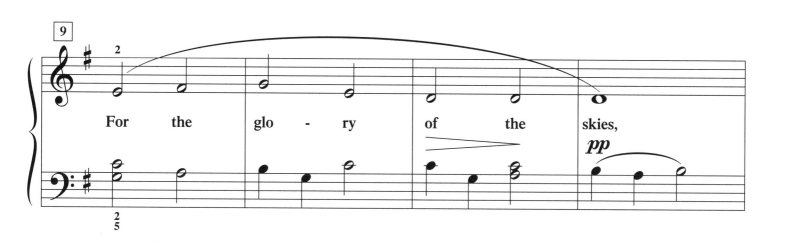

FJH2144

30

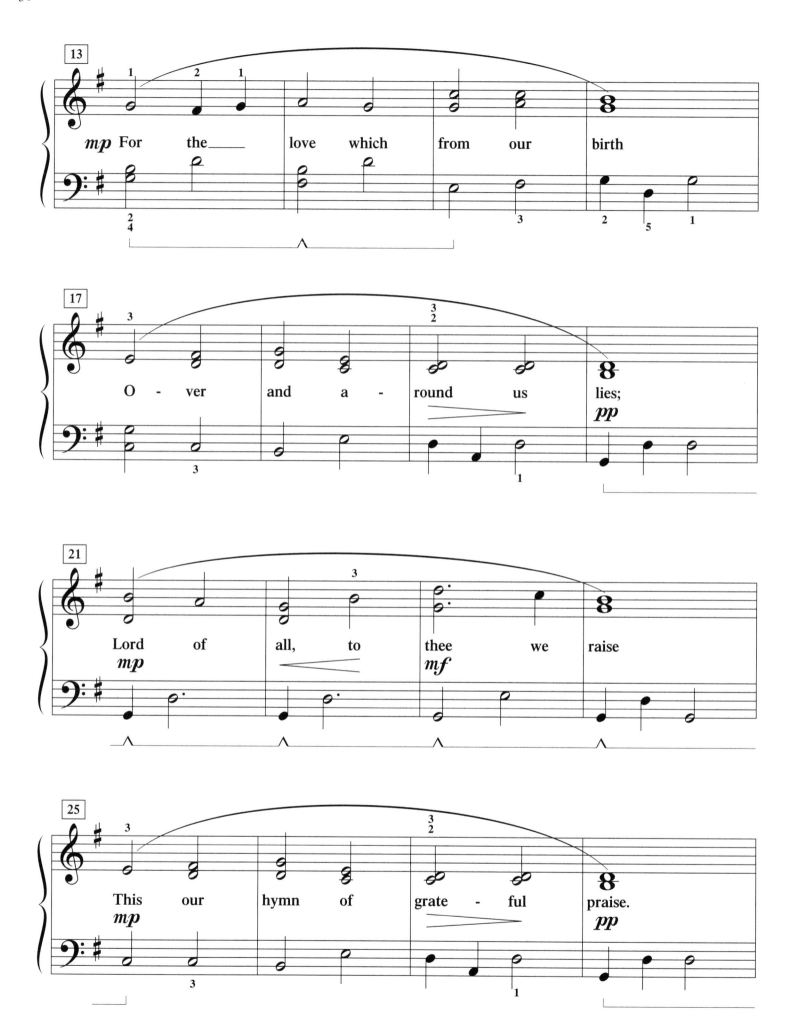

FJH2144

Poor Wayfaring Stranger
Secondo

Traditional Spiritual
arr. Kevin Olson

Poor Wayfaring Stranger
Primo

Traditional Spiritual
arr. Kevin Olson

Secondo

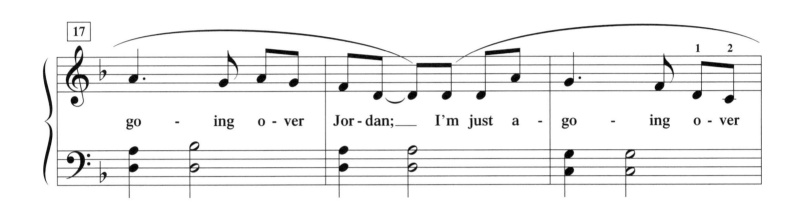

Primo

fa - ther,___ I'm go - ing home, no more to roam.

I'm go-ing

Secondo

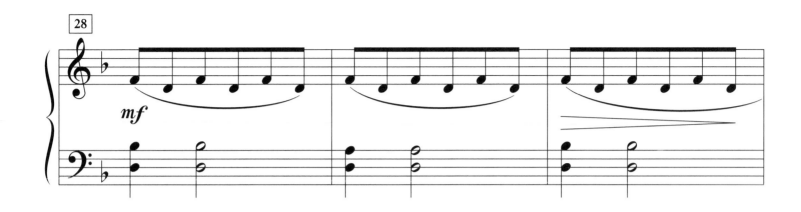

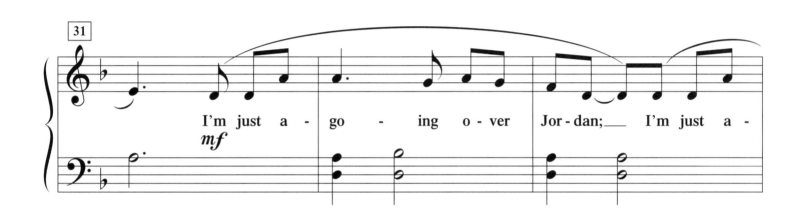

I'm just a - go - ing o - ver Jor - dan;___ I'm just a -

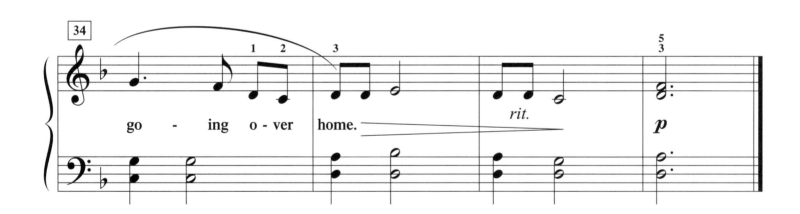

go - ing o - ver home.

Primo

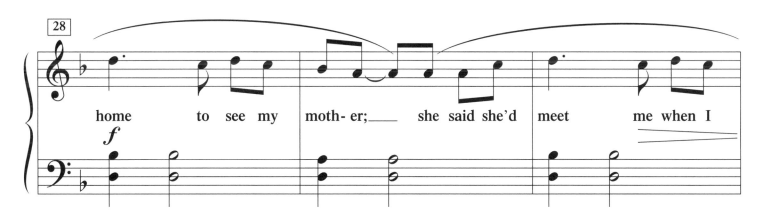

home   to see my   moth- er;____   she said she'd   meet   me when I

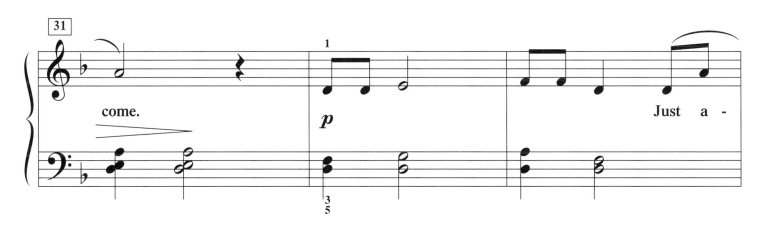

come.   Just a -

go - ing o - ver   home.____   *rit.*

Amazing Grace

Music from *Virginia Harmony*
Lyrics by John Newton
arr. Edwin McLean

2. 'Twas grace that taught my heart to fear,
   And grace my fears relieved;
   How precious did that grace appear,
   The hour I first believed.

ABOUT THE PIECES AND COMPOSERS

Just a Closer Walk with Thee

There is a tradition in New Orleans that is found nowhere else: the jazz funeral procession. Family and friends form a parade to transport the coffin toward the cemetery as a marching brass band plays very slowly and mournfully—often the anonymous song *Just a Closer Walk with Thee* or perhaps *Nearer, My God, to Thee*. Then while returning from the cemetery, the band plays faster, happier music like *When the Saints Go Marching In*.

Just a Closer Walk with Thee has been recorded by hundreds of musicians, including many that your grandparents and their parents liked to listen to: Red Foley, Elvis Presley, Tennessee Ernie Ford, Patti Page, The Blind Boys of Alabama, and many others.

God Be with You

Around the world, when people leave each other their parting words or phrases often contain a prayer or blessing. For example, the French say "adieu" which literally means "to God"—an abbreviation for "I entrust you to God." Likewise, in Spanish the word is "adios" which also means "to God." In English, we say "goodbye" which is an abbreviation of "God be with you." Jeremiah Rankin (1828-1904), a Congregational minister in Washington, D.C., felt the need for a goodbye hymn, and so in 1880 he wrote the lyrics for *God Be with You*. He then sent them across town to his friend William Tomer, who wrote a melody to fit the words. Later, Rankin became president of Howard University, and his hymn became a favorite song of "farewell" (another parting term containing a blessing).

What Wondrous Love Is This

What Wondrous Love Is This is a very old American song which was passed along from singer to singer for many years. It was first captured on paper in 1835, when it appeared in a collection of hymns called *Southern Harmony*. The melody sounds cool and mysterious because it's in the Dorian mode, a scale that is neither major nor minor. You could make up other interesting Dorian songs by improvising from D to D without using any black keys.

Rock of Ages

Augustus Toplady was born in 1740 in England. His father, a major in the British army, was killed the following year in a battle. His widowed mother then moved the family to Dublin, Ireland.

Toplady was educated at Trinity College and then ordained by the Church of England at the age of twenty-two. He soon began to show symptoms of

ABOUT THE PIECES AND COMPOSERS

tuberculosis. *Rock of Ages* first appeared in 1776 in the *Gospel Magazine,* of which Toplady was editor. His most famous writing effort turned out to be his last song; within two years tuberculosis claimed his life, and he died at the age of only thirty-eight.

For the Beauty of the Earth

Folliott Pierpoint (1835-1917), an Englishman, loved to walk through the woods or along beaches and enjoy the beauties of nature. Whenever he wasn't in a classroom at Somersetshire College, where he taught literature, he would sit outdoors and compose poems, many of which were later published in magazines. His most famous poem, *For the Beauty of the Earth,* first appeared in the 1864 hymn collection, *Lyra Eucharista,* where it was combined with a tune that had been written in 1838 by a German musician, Conrad Kocher (1786-1872).

Poor Wayfaring Stranger

This anonymous spiritual/folk song describes life as a long journey on foot, with rugged trails and frequent storms. It speaks of the Jordan River as the boundary between this earthly life and a heavenly reward, where the weary traveler will be reunited with family members who have already made the crossing.

This song has been sung by hundreds of recording artists, including Alison Krauss, Dolly Parton, Dusty Springfield, Johnny Cash, and Kristen Chenoweth.

Amazing Grace

John Newton was, by anyone's standards including his own, a very bad man. Born in London in 1725, as a young child he was very devoted to his mother. But when he was seven, she died of tuberculosis and John's world turned upside down. He became a very mean boy and did everything he could think of to get into trouble. At eighteen he became a sailor and kidnapped people from Africa to take to England and America as slaves. On one trip across the ocean he became so bored that he read a book called *The Imitation of Christ,* which reminded him how evil he really was. Later in that same voyage, a violent storm nearly sank the ship, bringing Newton to his knees. He promised God that if he survived he would turn his life around and become a good person. And can you believe it—a few years later he became a minister, a crusader against slavery, and a hymn writer! Throughout his long life, he teamed up with men like William Wilberforce and John Wesley to bring about many social reforms in England. Finally, in March of 1807 the English Parliament passed a law abolishing the British slave trade. Later that same year, the eighty-two year old Newton died. If ever there was a "wretch" who was "saved," it was that kidnapper who turned into a minister!

ABOUT THE ARRANGERS

Nancy Lau

Nancy Lau (pronounced "Law") has often been told that her music sounds very lyrical and natural. She discovered her love and talent for music early in life. Born with perfect pitch, by age four Nancy was able to play nursery rhymes on the piano by ear. She was soon coming up with her own arrangements of songs and was able to copy any music that she heard.

An active composer, arranger, and piano teacher, Nancy studied music composition with Dr. Norman Weston and piano pedagogy with Nakyong Chai at Saddleback College in Orange County, California. In addition to writing for piano, she has composed for solo voice and chamber ensemble, and has written many choral works. Her compositions have won numerous awards. Nancy maintains a full piano studio, where her emphasis is on keeping music enjoyable and exciting. She believes that students must feel nurtured and accepted, and strives to generate in her piano lessons a joyful experience and positive memory.

Edwin McLean

Edwin McLean is a composer living in Chapel Hill, North Carolina. He is a graduate of the Yale School of Music, where he studied with Krzysztof Penderecki and Jacob Druckman. He also holds a master's degree in music theory and a bachelor's degree in piano performance from the University of Colorado.

Mr. McLean has authored over 200 publications for The FJH Music Company, ranging from *The FJH Classic Music Dictionary* to original works for pianists from beginner to advanced. His highly-acclaimed works for harpsichord have been performed internationally and are available on the Miami Bach Society recording, *Edwin McLean: Sonatas for 1, 2, and 3 Harpsichords*. His 2011 solo jazz piano album *Don't Say Goodbye* (CD1043) includes many of his advanced works for piano published by FJH.

Edwin McLean began his career as a professional arranger. Currently, he is senior editor for The FJH Music Company Inc.

Kevin Olson

Kevin Olson is an active pianist, composer, and member of the piano faculty at Utah State University, where he teaches piano literature, pedagogy, and accompanying courses. In addition to his collegiate teaching responsibilities, Kevin directs the Utah State Youth Conservatory, which provides weekly group and private piano instruction to more than 200 pre-college community students. The National Association of Schools of Music has recently recognized the Conservatory as a model for pre-college piano instruction programs. Before teaching at Utah State, he was on the faculty at Elmhurst College near Chicago and Humboldt State University in northern California.

A native of Utah, Kevin began composing at age five. When he was twelve, his composition, *An American Trainride*, received the Overall First Prize at the 1983 National PTA Convention at Albuquerque, New Mexico. Since then he has been a Composer in Residence at the National Conference on Piano Pedagogy, and has written music commissioned and performed by groups such as the American Piano Quartet, Chicago a cappella, the Rich Matteson Jazz Festival, and several piano teacher associations around the country.

Kevin maintains a large piano studio, teaching students of a variety of ages and abilities. Many of the needs of his own piano students have inspired more than 100 books and solos published by the FJH Music Company, which he joined as a writer in 1994.

ABOUT THE ARRANGERS

Valerie Roth Roubos

Valerie Roth Roubos earned degrees in music theory, composition, and flute performance from the University of Wyoming. Ms. Roubos maintains a studio in her home in Spokane, Washington, where she teaches flute, piano, and composition.

Active as a performer, adjudicator, lecturer, and accompanist, Ms. Roubos has lectured and taught master classes at the Washington State Music Teachers Conference, Holy Names Music Camp, and the Spokane and Tri-Cities chapters of Washington State Music Teachers Association. She has played an active role in the Spokane Music Teachers Association and WSMTA.

In 2001, the South Dakota Music Teachers Association selected Ms. Roubos as Composer of the Year, and with MTNA commissioned her to write *An American Portrait: Scenes from the Great Plains*, published by The FJH Music Company Inc. Ms. Roubos was chosen to be the 2004–2005 composer-in-residence at Washington State University. In 2006, WSMTA selected her as Composer of the Year. Ms. Roubos' teaching philosophy and compositions reflect her belief that all students, from elementary to advanced, are capable of musical playing that incorporates sensitivity and expression. Her compositions represent a variety of musical styles, including sacred, choral, and educational piano works.

Robert Schultz

Robert Schultz, composer, arranger, and editor, has achieved international fame during his career in the music publishing industry. The Schultz Piano Library, established in 1980, has included more than 500 publications of classical works, popular arrangements, and Schultz's original compositions in editions for pianists of every level from the beginner through the concert artist. In addition to his extensive library of published piano works, Schultz's output includes original orchestral works, chamber music, works for solo instruments, and vocal music.

Schultz has presented his published editions at workshops, clinics, and convention showcases throughout the United States and Canada. He is a long-standing member of ASCAP and has served as president of the Miami Music Teachers Association. Mr. Schultz's original piano compositions and transcriptions are featured on the compact disc recordings *Visions of Dunbar* and *Tina Faigen Plays Piano Transcriptions*, released on the ACA Digital label and available worldwide. His published original works for concert artists are noted in Maurice Hinson's *Guide to the Pianist's Repertoire, Third Edition*. He currently devotes his full time to composing and arranging. In-depth information about Robert Schultz and The Schultz Piano Library is available at the Website www.schultzmusic.com.

USING THE CD

A great way to prepare for your recitals is to listen to the CD.

Enjoy listening to these wonderful pieces anywhere anytime! Listen to them casually (as background music) and attentively. After you have listened to the CD you might discuss interpretation with your teacher and follow along with your score as you listen.

HYMN PERFORMANCES

Hymns	Where Played	Date	Special Memory of the Event
Onward Christian Soldiers			
I Need Thee Every Hour			
We Gather Together			
Praise to the Lord, the Almighty			
Shall We Gather at the River			
Just a Closer Walk with Thee			
God Be with You			
What Wondrous Love Is This			
Rock of Ages			
For the Beauty of the Earth			
Poor Wayfaring Sranger			
Amazing Grace			